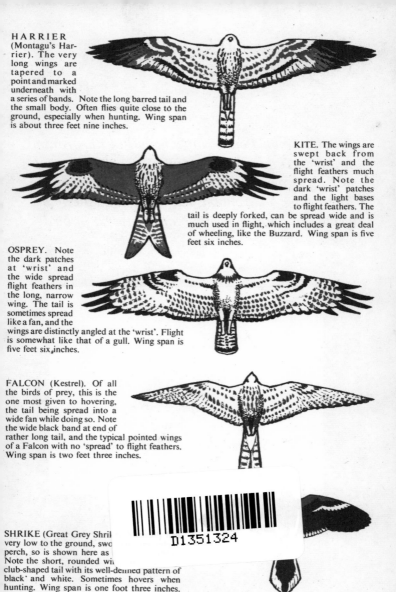

HARRIER (Montagu's Harrier). The very long wings are tapered to a point and marked underneath with a series of bands. Note the long barred tail and the small body. Often flies quite close to the ground, especially when hunting. Wing span is about three feet nine inches.

KITE. The wings are swept back from the 'wrist' and the flight feathers much spread. Note the dark 'wrist' patches and the light bases to flight feathers. The tail is deeply forked, can be spread wide and is much used in flight, which includes a great deal of wheeling, like the Buzzard. Wing span is five feet six inches.

OSPREY. Note the dark patches at 'wrist' and the wide spread flight feathers in the long, narrow wing. The tail is sometimes spread like a fan, and the wings are distinctly angled at the 'wrist'. Flight is somewhat like that of a gull. Wing span is five feet six inches.

FALCON (Kestrel). Of all the birds of prey, this is the one most given to hovering, the tail being spread into a wide fan while doing so. Note the wide black band at end of rather long tail, and the typical pointed wings of a Falcon with no 'spread' to flight feathers. Wing span is two feet three inches.

SHRIKE (Great Grey Shrike very low to the ground, swo perch, so is shown here as Note the short, rounded wit club-shaped tail with its well-defined pattern of black and white. Sometimes hovers when hunting. Wing span is one foot three inches.

A Ladybird Nature Book
Series 536

*John Leigh-Pemberton's beautiful illustrations
will help children—and adults—to identify
any birds of prey they might see. The clear,
interesting and reliable text will stimulate many
people to take an even greater interest in bird
life.*

HOLIDAY DIARY 1972

3rd YEAR PRIZE

Abigail   Wedmore

BIRDS OF PREY

by
JOHN LEIGH-PEMBERTON

Publishers: Wills & Hepworth Ltd., Loughborough
First published 1970   ©   *Printed in England*

Barn Owl*

Owls are to a great extent nocturnal birds; that is, they are active and hunt for their food at night although not usually in total darkness. Like other nocturnal creatures, they have enormous eyes, almost as large as a man's, but for hunting they depend even more on their very acute sense of hearing. For this purpose they have specially adapted ears.

The food of all Owls consists of live animal prey such as insects, birds, mice, rats. The bigger the Owl the bigger the prey, and very large Owls will take rabbits and hares. They swoop upon their prey from above, killing it with their powerful talons. Prey is eaten whole—skin, bones, etc., but the indigestible parts are coughed up later in the form of pellets.

The Barn Owl prefers the vicinity of farms or other buildings, and also inhabits cliffs. It is not found everywhere, but is distributed in suitable places throughout the British Isles, with the exception of northern Scotland, where it is only rarely found.

The usual cry is a drawn-out, rather frightening shriek, sometimes uttered in flight, and hissing and loud snoring noises are also heard. The Barn Owl can live for as long as fifteen years or more.

Barn Owls usually nest in empty buildings or in hollow trees. From four to seven eggs are laid, sometimes very early in the year and sometimes very late. There is no real attempt to make a nest, and no nesting materials are used.

4

7214 0259 3   *See also ' Garden Birds' in this series*

INDEX

Tawny Owl or Brown Owl*

The eyes of Owls, like those of many creatures which are hunters, face forwards. This gives them the sort of vision that Man has (called 'binocular vision'), which includes the ability to judge distances very accurately. However, the eyes of an Owl are so large that they can hardly move in their sockets, as ours can, so it has to be able to turn its head right round, through 180 degrees, in order to increase its field of vision. This means that although Owls appear to have very short necks, they have, in fact, longer and more flexible necks than most birds.

The commonest English Owl is the Tawny Owl, which is found throughout Great Britain but not in Ireland. It is less common in the western counties and rare in northern Scotland. The favoured habitat is almost anywhere where there are plenty of big trees, and it will live quite happily in suburban gardens or in town parks. Tawny Owls nest in hollow trees or in the disused nests of other birds or squirrels. Occasionally they nest in farm buildings, or on the ground, or even in a nesting-box made of half a barrel and placed in a tree. No nesting material is used, and the single brood consists of from two to four eggs.

Food is the same as for other Owls, but the Tawny Owl will eat shrews, which some birds of prey will not. Two cries are typical—the familiar 'hoo-hoo-hoo' and, even more often, 'kewick'.

6

Little Owl

Although it is now a resident bird, the Little Owl was known here only as an uncommon visitor until the end of the nineteenth century. However, in 1889 it was introduced from Holland, and has established itself and bred here since then. It is uncommon in Scotland and Ireland, and really belongs to the southern half of England and Wales.

The Little Owl is a very small bird (8–9 inches), with a very large head. Because of the feather formation above its eyes, it wears what appears to be a perpetual frown. It hunts mostly at dusk and dawn, but is often seen perched in full view in daylight on telegraph poles, posts or walls. Here it sits bobbing up and down and turning its head in all directions. It eats a great many insects and a few mice, but is less likely to take small birds. It can, however, tackle a bird of its own size, such as a starling. It often kills more food than it can eat at once.

The usual cry is a rather shrill 'kiu'.

Little Owls like open country, such as farmland with plenty of hedges. They nest in hollow trees, on buildings, or even in rabbit burrows, and occasionally in the old nests of other birds. Three to five eggs are laid and, as with other Owls, these are incubated for about a month by the hen alone. Both parents feed the chicks, and sometimes there are two broods.

Long-Eared Owl

Several kinds of Owls throughout the world have little tufts of feathers springing from their heads, just above the eyes. These are nothing to do with their ears which are placed, as with other birds, at the side of the head. The so-called ear tufts are not always visible, and in flight are usually laid flat.

The Long-Eared Owl is a resident bird, found in some localities throughout Britain and particularly in Ireland. It favours plantations of pine or spruce, but is sometimes found in mixed woodland or on heaths or sand dunes. Of all British Owls it is the most nocturnal and is rarely seen by day. In winter some migrant birds arrive in eastern England from the continent, but generally the Long-Eared Owl is decreasing in Britain.

As with other Owls, the eggs are white and almost round. Four or five are laid in March or April, usually in the old nest of a Magpie or Crow but sometimes on the ground at the foot of a tree. Only the hen incubates, and there is only one brood. In winter or on migration, small parties are sometimes formed, but generally this is a solitary bird.

Food is the same as for other British Owls. The cry, or 'song', consists of a repeated moaning sound 'oo-oo-oo'. The young, in particular, utter yelping and whining noises very similar to those made by a dog.

Short-Eared Owl

This interesting Owl is a bird of the open country and is found mostly in Scotland, northern England and East Anglia. It is a resident breeding bird in Britain, but part of our population is made up of winter migrant birds from the continent. It lives mainly on the ground, inhabiting marshes, dunes and heathland, and is most active in daylight, hunting and flying on its long wings much more in the manner of a hawk than an Owl. It occasionally soars to considerable heights, but its normal flight is close to the ground.

The 'ear-tufts' are hardly visible, and disappear when the bird is excited and raises its other feathers. The cry when angry is a harsh 'kwowk', and the song a low, repeated 'boo-boo-boo' sometimes uttered in flight.

This bird lives chiefly on voles, and the population of Short-Eared Owls and the number of eggs they lay is governed by the availability of their food supply. Thus, in a year when voles are numerous and form a 'plague', the number of Short-Eared Owls increases. In these years as many as a dozen eggs are laid, and there may be two broods. Normally there is one brood of from four to eight eggs. These are laid in a scraped-out hollow on the ground, and the young, hatched by the hen alone, leave the nest a week earlier than other Owls—in about fifteen days.

Snowy Owl

The flight of Owls is remarkably silent, and this is due to their exceptionally long and soft feathers. A double purpose is achieved by this—the prey cannot hear the Owl's approach, and the Owl itself can hear its prey more easily.

Even the very large Snowy Owl flies silently, and its soft, white plumage keeps it warm in the Arctic climate from which it comes.

The female, as with most Owls, is larger than the male and her plumage is more barred than his. These Owls have feathered feet and, in common with all Owls, the outer toe can be made to point backwards.

Up to a few years ago, the Snowy Owl was only an occasional winter visitor to Shetland, the Hebrides and northern Scotland. Since 1967, however, a pair has bred every year on Fetlar, an island in the Shetland group. The nest is on the ground, on a hillock from which the bird can overlook the surrounding country. The usual cry, not often heard, is 'krow-ow' or 'rick-rick'.

During summer in the Snowy Owl's home in the Arctic there is practically no night, so this Owl has become a daylight hunter, taking prey as large as hares, and hunting and flying in a manner very like that of a Buzzard. It will also catch fish, using its powerful feet to hook them out of the water.

Golden Eagle

The Golden Eagle is resident in the Highlands of Scotland, the Hebrides and occasionally in a few other parts of Scotland and Ireland. Elsewhere it is extremely rare and is declining in numbers. This is partly due to the fact that the Eagle, in common with many other birds of prey, eats birds and mammals which have been poisoned by the chemical sprays used for protecting crops. These may not only kill the bird itself, but reduce its ability to breed, and thus many species of birds of prey are gravely threatened.

The majestic, soaring flight, the great size of talons, bill and wings are the features for which the Eagle is noted. It is not as bold as an Owl or a Falcon, and does not live by hunting alone, being also a carrion eater. It hunts grouse, ptarmigan and blue hares, usually swooping on them from above.

Golden Eagles inhabit wild, mountainous country, and generally nest on a crag or rock ledge. The nest, or 'eyrie', used year after year, is a huge structure made of branches and lined with heather and bracken. It is decorated with fresh pine branches. Here one brood of two eggs is laid, one egg nearly always white and the other heavily spotted with colour. The hen hatches the chicks, but both parents feed them. It is eleven weeks before they can fly.

The Eagle's cry is a sharp yelp or a whistle, but it is a somewhat silent bird.

Buzzard

In south-west England, Wales and western Scotland, the Buzzard is still a fairly common bird, but since the decrease in the rabbit population (due to disease) in about 1954, it has become scarcer. The deadly effect of poisonous crop sprays has also affected it.

Buzzards are intermediate in size between Eagles and the larger Hawks, with which they have much in common. They are capable of soaring to great heights on almost motionless wings, wheeling round in large circles for hours on end. Occasionally they hover or dive. When hunting they fly fairly low, pouncing on their prey from above and catching small mammals and only occasional birds or insects. Carrion is also eaten.

The type of country favoured is mountain, moorland or heavily wooded agricultural areas. Here the Buzzard builds a large nest in a tree or on a cliff face. It is made of sticks or heather and lined with moss and grass. The hen decorates the nest with sprays of pine, ivy or even seaweed, replacing it when it withers.

The single brood is incubated and raised by both parents, and usually two or three eggs are laid, often at widely spaced intervals. For this reason, the young in a nest are often of differing ages, and the older chicks tend to starve out the younger ones. In addition, as a high proportion of Buzzards' eggs are infertile, the number of surviving young is probably no more than one from each nest.

Rough-Legged Buzzard

Whereas the resident common Buzzard inhabits westerly parts of Britain, the Rough-Legged Buzzard—a winter visitor only—is found in eastern Scotland and the coastal or hilly areas of north-east England. It is not a common bird, and is not often seen, for it prefers desolate places such as marshes, moors or hills.

The name 'Rough-Legged' is earned by its feathered legs, which other Buzzards do not possess. Like all Buzzards, its plumage is soft like that of Owls and is extremely variable. Almost white specimens have been recorded as well as very dark ones, but generally the white head and underparts are typical. The best way of distinguishing Buzzards from each other is by noticing the pattern under the tail (see end-papers).

This bird breeds in Scandinavia and in Russia. In common with other birds of prey, the female is larger than the male. The cry is very similar to that of the Buzzard—a mewing sound, drawn out and rather like the cry of a gull—'pee-iou'. The flight is typical of Buzzards, but the Rough-Legged species is much more given to hovering in the manner of the smaller hawks.

In the past Buzzards have been ruthlessly and needlessly persecuted by game-keepers and farmers, who have shot them and destroyed their eggs. In fact, they kill very few birds of any kind, but do much good by destroying rabbits, rats and other vermin.

Honey Buzzard *(hen above, cock below)*

The Honey Buzzard is rather different from the Buzzard and the Rough-Legged Buzzard. It is a smaller bird which spends much time on the ground and has feeding habits rather unusual for a bird of prey. The Honey Buzzard eats great quantities of insects, especially the grubs of wasps and bees. From its habit of digging out and destroying wasps' or bees' nests, it used to be believed that it ate honey—hence its name. It will occasionally soar like other Buzzards and, like them, will hunt and kill small mammals, birds and reptiles.

This bird is a rather uncommon visitor, coming to us as it migrates between the continent, where it breeds, and tropical Africa, where it spends the winter. Very occasionally it nests here, usually in southern and eastern England, and in most years specimens are seen.

It favours country with open woodland, particularly large areas of beech or pine, and like many birds of prey it is much given to perching—high up and absolutely stationary—for long periods at a time. When doing so, it is—like all birds of prey—frequently mobbed and scolded by flocks of smaller birds.

Honey Buzzards are rather silent, but have a characteristic cry 'pika' or 'ki-ha'.

In May or June two or three eggs are laid, either in the deserted nest of some other bird or in a small nest built and decorated by the parent birds. Both cock and hen incubate and feed the young.

Kite

Only in central Wales is it now possible to see a Kite in Britain, but a century ago it bred in many parts of England. In Elizabethan times it was common in the streets of London, where it acted as a scavenger. Foreign travellers used to remark on the sight of the many Kites wheeling, like Buzzards, over the city. Now there are about twenty breeding pairs in Wales, and perhaps a very few others elsewhere. Wooded valleys among hills are the areas it favours.

The Kite's cry, 'hi-hi-hiah', is a high-pitched mewing, and it is very noisy at breeding times. The nest is usually in the fork of an oak tree, elaborately made of sticks packed with earth and lined with moss, hair, wool and even rags and pieces of paper. Two or three eggs are laid, incubated by the hen alone for thirty days. The young fly when about fifty days old.

Food consists largely of carrion, but Kites hunt, like Buzzards, and catch rabbits and birds on the ground.

One of the reasons for the Kite's rarity is that in the past collectors took their eggs. It is now illegal to kill or capture any wild birds or to take their eggs (with special exceptions). The penalties are up to five pounds for each egg of a common bird, and twenty-five pounds for a rare one. It is, of course, quite wrong to collect them at all.

Marsh Harrier *(cock above, hen below)*

With most birds of prey the hen is larger than the cock, but with the Marsh Harrier the hen is also of very different plumage. With all three British species of Harrier, the cock has some grey in his plumage—the hen none.

Harriers have long tails, wings and bodies, and their legs are longer than those of other Hawks. Their wings are tapered to a point and, in flight, beat slowly or are half spread in a glide. They fly, head down, backwards and forwards a few feet above the ground as they search for prey. At other times—for instance, in the breeding season—they fly at considerable heights.

The Marsh Harrier breeds in small numbers in Norfolk, Suffolk, North Wales and southern England, but it is usually only a summer visitor and very few birds spend the winter here. Perhaps no more than twenty pairs of this rare bird come to us each year.

Food, taken by pouncing on it from above, consists of small mammals and birds which inhabit the reed beds where this bird is found.

The large nest, built by the hen, is among growing reeds and constructed well above the water with dead reeds and water plants. Curiously enough, the cock builds a second nest from which further nesting material is taken to the hen as she incubates the four or five eggs.

The rare cry is a soft 'kee-oo'.

Hen Harrier (*cock above, hen below*)

The Hen Harrier is a little smaller and slimmer than the Marsh Harrier, and is found in the Orkneys where it is a breeding resident. A few pairs breed in the Outer Hebrides, in south-west Ireland and locally on the Scottish mainland. Elsewhere it occurs occasionally as a migrant or a winter visitor. It is essentially a bird of wild moorland, but in winter visits farmland, fens or sand dunes.

This bird hunts in a typically Harrier-like fashion, flying low over the ground, which is thoroughly searched. Small mammals and birds are pounced on from above. The cry is a chattering 'ke-ke-kek', usually uttered near the nest.

Four or five eggs are laid in May, in a thickly-lined nest built by the hen on the ground and decorated by her with heather or birch sprays. The hen, often called a 'ring-tail', does all the incubating, hatching out the chicks in about thirty days; they leave the nest thirty-nine days later. As with all Harriers, the feeding of the sitting hen and the young is a fascinating sight. The cock finds the food and flies over, calling the hen from the nest. She flies up to him and the food is transferred from foot to foot in flight. Sometimes it is dropped by the cock and caught by the hen.

A very similar bird, known as the Marsh Hawk, is common in North America.

Montagu's Harrier (*cock above, hen below*)

The smallest of our Harriers is the slim, dashing and elegant Montagu's Harrier, distinguished as far as the cock is concerned by the dark bar across the middle wing. This bar is absent in the cock Hen Harrier. Although they appear to be sizeable birds on account of their large wing span, Harriers have not the stout build of some birds of prey such as Buzzards. They measure only from seventeen inches long (Montagu's) to about twenty-one inches (Marsh Harrier). A cock Montagu's Harrier weighs only nine or ten ounces, although the larger hen may weigh as much as fourteen ounces.

Another point to notice about Harriers is that, like Owls, they have round faces edged with a faint outline of projecting feathers. They are found almost everywhere in the world except the Polar regions, the Pacific Islands and New Zealand.

The feeding and nesting habits of Montagu's Harrier are the same as those of the Hen Harrier, and the cry 'yick-yick-yick' is similar but softer. It likes open heaths, especially with gorse bushes or marshes. At times it hunts over agricultural land, and is more inclined to eat frogs and snakes than are other Harriers.

This bird visits England in small numbers in the summer, but is uncommon in Scotland and Ireland. About twenty pairs breed between south-west England and the New Forest, but unfortunately the numbers are decreasing. In winter our visitors migrate to Africa.

Sparrow-hawk (*cock above, hen below*)

The Hawk family of birds of prey is made up of the Buzzards, the Harriers, the Kite, the Eagle and the two smaller hawks—the Sparrow-hawk and the Goshawk. All have blunt or rounded wings and yellowish or brownish eyes.

Of these the Sparrow-hawk is the smallest, the cock being very much smaller than the hen and, like the three species of Harrier, very different in plumage. This was once a common resident bird found everywhere except in the most northerly part of Britain. Its numbers have now decreased very seriously and suddenly, partly through the destruction of its habitat—the hedgerow and small copse—but principally as the result of the use of poisonous chemicals on crops. These have the effect of poisoning the food of birds of prey.

Small mammals, birds and insects form its diet, for which it hunts in a very characteristic manner, dashing along the edge of a wood or from side to side of a hedgerow. Birds are captured by sheer speed of man-oeuvre. The chattering cry—usually in alarm—is 'kek-kek-kek'.

Sparrow-hawks lay a single clutch of four or five eggs in a nest situated in a tree—pine, spruce or larch being preferred. Sometimes the old nest of some other bird is taken over and improved upon, usually by the hen alone. She also does all the incubation and feeds the chicks, although the cock provides the food.

Goshawk

Very occasionally the Goshawk breeds in Britain, usually in the south-east of England. Recently it seems to have settled as a resident bird, but in very small numbers. Generally speaking, it is a somewhat rare visitor, coming here from the continent where it is a resident species and normally breeds. This bird is like a large, very powerful version of a female Sparrow-hawk, and of all the Hawks (as opposed to Falcons) was the one most prized by falconers. Used for this sport mainly in wooded country, it could catch large prey such as rabbits. It is possible that some of the Goshawks seen in this country are modern falconers' birds which have escaped.

In spite of its size, a Goshawk can thread its way very rapidly through thick woodland, turning and twisting on its broad wings. It nests in wooded country, either in the discarded nest of some other bird, such as a crow, or in one of its own making. This is built by the hen, close to the trunk of a stout tree, and is made of sticks with a lining of twigs and greenery. There is one brood of three or four eggs which are incubated by both parents (but mainly by the hen) and hatch out in about thirty-six days. Forty-five days later the chicks leave the nest, although still unable to fly.

Goshawks are rather silent birds, but have a typical hawk-like alarm note—'kek-kek', loud and rapid.

Osprey

The Osprey is different from other British birds of prey, chiefly because it is always found in the vicinity of water. Although it has much of the appearance of a Hawk or Eagle, its feathers are much more like those of some Vultures. Its feet, with outer toes which can be pointed backwards, are more like those of an Owl and enable it to catch and carry the fish upon which it lives almost entirely.

Found almost throughout the world, the Osprey was only a rare, wandering visitor in Britain until recently, although a few were seen in most years. Since 1954, however, one or two pairs have nested each year near Loch Garten in Inverness-shire, and in 1959 the eggs, protected against collectors, were successfully hatched and the young reared.

Ospreys have a sharp, whistling cry. They nest on an island or in the tops of pine trees, building a large nest of sticks and other materials. Both birds share in the building, and the same nest is used year after year. Two or three eggs are laid and usually incubated by the hen only. There is one brood.

Their method of hunting is to fly over the water, sometimes hovering at about a hundred feet up. When a fish is sighted near the surface, the Osprey plunges, grasping the fish with its talons and then rising with it from the water.

Greenland Gyrfalcon

Falcons form a family of birds of prey which are distinguished by their long, pointed wings, thick shoulders and heads larger than those of Hawks. They have fairly long tails and dark, very beautiful eyes which are often surrounded by patches of yellow skin. In many species of Falcon, the cock and hen are quite different in plumage. The hen is larger than the cock.

Falcons vary in size from the little Merlin, which is about ten and a half inches long (cock), to the Gyrfalcon, which can be twenty-four inches long (hen). All are hunters which usually catch their prey in mid-air but sometimes on the ground. They are among the swiftest birds in the world; in pursuit of prey, stooping or diving, some Falcons have been recorded at speeds of more than 150 m.p.h. They are complete masters of flight in every sort of manoeuvre. The cry is a loud 'kyak'.

There are three species of the Gyrfalcon, all rare in Britain. The commonest of these winter visitors from Arctic regions and northern Europe is the Greenland Gyrfalcon, which occasionally visits Scotland and northern England. The Iceland Gyrfalcon, a greyer bird, more heavily marked, is even rarer, and the European Gyrfalcon from Scandinavia has not been seen here for a century. It is like a large Peregrine.

Although rare and difficult to train, Gyrfalcons were much prized by falconers for flying at larger game. Their food includes ptarmigan, gulls, hares and lemmings.

Peregrine

Perhaps the most perfect of all Falcons is the Peregrine. This bird lives on sea cliffs or moorland, but in winter comes inland; sometimes it breeds even on high buildings in towns.

Peregrines are resident throughout Britain, although they do not normally breed in the Midlands or south-east England. It is not a common bird, having been persecuted by gamekeepers in the past because it takes gamebirds, particularly Grouse. Since 1955 it has become even rarer, its numbers much reduced by the use of poisonous chemicals on farmland.

Prey is taken in full flight by a spectacular dive from above, with wings half folded. Sea birds and pigeons form the greater part of the Peregrine's diet, but it may occasionally include mammals as large as rabbits. During nesting the cock feeds the hen by passing food to her in the air, either from foot to foot or by dropping it for her to catch. Only in the breeding season is the cry much heard—a shrill chatter, 'kek-kek-kek' and 'kwark-kwark'—almost a quacking noise.

The nest may be in a rabbit hole or on a crag, or sometimes in the discarded nest of another bird. No nesting material is used. Three or four eggs are laid in April, and both parents incubate. There is only one brood.

This bird was the favourite of falconers, who refer to the hen as the 'falcon' and the cock as the 'tiercel'.

Hobby

Slimmer and smaller than the Peregrine, the Hobby has the longest wings of all our Falcons. In level flight (as opposed to stooping or diving) it may well be the fastest flyer among our birds of prey; it can fly through a flock of House Martins and seize one without hesitating. It is said to be particularly fond of taking Skylarks, but a great proportion of its diet undoubtedly consists of the larger insects such as beetles. These are caught and eaten on the wing, often in semi-darkness.

This migratory bird is more common in continental Europe than in Britain. The breeding population in this country is probably fewer than a hundred pairs. These are mainly concentrated, in summer, in Hampshire and the adjoining counties, with a few pairs in the area of the Welsh Border. In winter the Hobby leaves for Africa at the same time as the Swallows.

In the breeding season, pairs perform wonderful aerobatics, often at a considerable height. No nest is built, but that of a Sparrow-hawk, Crow or squirrel is taken over and three eggs are laid. There is only one brood, incubated chiefly by the hen for about twenty-eight days. Both parents feed the chicks, and during incubation the cock feeds the hen by passing food to her in the air, as with the Peregrine and the Harriers.

Farmland, downland and woodland are the most favoured habitats. Here can be heard the high-pitched cry 'dew-dew-dew', or the usual 'kek' note of other Falcons.

Kestrel *(cock above, hen below)*

The Kestrel is by far the most common of our Hawks and Falcons. It is a resident bird and is found throughout Britain, with the exception of the Shetlands. Like other birds of prey, it has decreased in numbers in recent years, but in spite of persecution by gamekeepers it is now becoming more common again. It is found mainly in moorland, woodland and coastal areas, and even in large towns, but is rarely seen in farming country.

A small bird of prey seen hovering is most likely to be a Kestrel, hunting for the mice or voles which, with insects and small birds, form its diet. Hovering is carried out head to wind, and one of the names for this bird is 'windhover'. Prey is caught by stooping, catching it on the ground, although some insects are caught in the air. Like most Falcons, the Kestrel's flight consists of a series of rapid, flickering wing beats, followed by a glide.

Sometimes the old nest of some other bird is used, sometimes a hollow in a tree or building or a ledge on a cliff-face. No nesting material is used, and the four or five eggs are laid in a roughly scraped-out hollow. Nesting takes place fairly early in the year, but there is only one brood, fed by both parents.

The Kestrel's cry is a loud 'kee-kee-kee' and sometimes 'kee-lee', a more musical double note.

Merlin *(cock left, hen right)*

In the days when falconry was popular, the pretty little Merlin was regarded as the 'Ladies' Falcon' because of its extreme lightness when it sat upon the wrist. The cock is not much bigger than a Blackbird and is smaller than the hen, which has very different plumage.

Merlins are found in wild, open country such as bare hills, moors or sea cliffs. As much of this country has been developed for forestry in recent years, the number of Merlins has declined. They are not found in south-east England but are resident breeding birds in Wales, the hilly parts of northern England, Scotland and parts of Ireland. A few pairs breed on Exmoor and Dartmoor.

The method of hunting is to fly low, occasionally hovering and suddenly pouncing upon small birds in the air by striking at them with the hind toe from above. Insects and small mammals are sometimes taken on the ground. Like many other birds of prey, the Merlin takes its prize to a regular perch, where it eats it. The cry of the cock is 'ki-ki-ki', but the hen has a lower, quite different cry—'eep-eep'.

The nest is often on the ground, particularly among heather. Sometimes old nests of other birds are used, but when making a new nest, the Merlin does make an attempt at building and lining. Four eggs are laid, and both cock and hen incubate the single brood.

Red-Backed Shrike or Butcher Bird
(cock above, hen below)

Shrikes are a family of perching birds found almost all over the world. They are not related to Owls, Hawks or Falcons, but their way of life is rather similar. They hunt and kill other birds, mice, frogs and insects, pouncing on them from a lofty perch from which the surrounding area can be watched. Prey is sometimes spiked on a thorn or secured in the fork of a branch, thus forming a store of food known as a 'larder'. This is quite often abandoned and left uneaten. Like Owls, Shrikes eat more of their prey than they can digest, and the indigestible parts are disgorged in the form of pellets.

All Shrikes are now rare in Britain, but the Red-Backed Shrike or Butcher Bird is sometimes seen in southern and eastern England in summer. It is very rare in Scotland and Ireland. The most favoured habitats are heathland and commons with thick bushes or hedgerows, and Shrikes are very fond of perching on telegraph wires in small family parties.

A large nest is built, usually by the cock, and placed fairly high up in a hedge or bush. It is well lined with hair, grass and moss. Four to six eggs are laid, and both parents incubate, the chicks hatching in about sixteen days.

Harsh 'clacking' noises are the normal cry, but rather surprisingly the cock has a low, quite musical song and is also a clever mimic of other birds.

Great Grey Shrike

The Great Grey Shrike is a rare autumn and winter visitor to the eastern side of Britain, coming to us from northern Europe. Although only nine and a half inches long, it is a powerful, aggressive bird which will kill other birds up to its own size and will even attack Hawks. Like all birds of prey, it is 'mobbed' by groups of smaller birds, who show their dislike of its presence by surrounding it as it perches, scolding it with noisy cries. The sound of 'mobbing', to which Blackbirds and Great Tits are particularly prone, is often a good indication of the presence of a bird of prey. Shrikes will themselves join in mobbing other birds such as Hawks and Owls.

The huge tail of the Great Grey Shrike is constantly wagged up and down as if to help the bird balance on its perch. The Shrike sits for long periods, only leaving a perch to catch prey or fly to another vantage point. Flight is very close to the ground, followed by a swoop upwards to a fresh perch. Sometimes it will hover like a Hawk, and its hunting methods are rather similar to those of the Hawk.

The Great Grey Shrike has a call rather like that of a Magpie, uttered mainly as an alarm note. The type of country in which it is sometimes seen is the same as that of the Red-Backed Shrike, but both birds are becoming increasingly uncommon.